Wander Where They Will

In Geneva the Birds

Á Genève les oiseaux n'ont pas peur
les oiseaux du monde entier
les chansons dans mon coeur
mes chansons cachées.
My hidden songs.

Songs of the first
last swan, dear.
At Siena, Saint Rose,
Thatcher Park or at Knapp's
with Rilke and Yeats, poetry

so inebriating, so savory—
licking the print off the page
in an homage to Keats
page by delicious page.
In Geneva the birds unafraid.

Intricate, love never ends—
in Albany birdstreets,
Jay and Lark and Dove.
All of the world entire,
I remember.

Wander Where They Will

Poems by Chuck Tripi

Cyberwit.net
HIG 45 Kaushambi Kunj, Kalindipuram
Allahabad - 211011 (U.P.) India
http://www.cyberwit.net
Tel: +(91) 9415091004
E-mail: info@cyberwit.net

Printed in India at VCORE CONNECT LLP.

For Finnian, Cavan and Kieran, Betsy and Susannah, Chris and James

and for our dear late grandmother, mother and wife, Barbara

Contents

May

After long sorrow, long happiness came.
When trees in the spring began flowering
each of the flowers was given a name,
the scent and the names intoxicating.
And then rivers ran and then poets sang.
In the valley was work for everyone.
Chop chop chops of the woodsmen, smithy *clangs*
pleased the hearers, and when the work was done
the chimneys smoked and the horses wore shoes
and the scent was good and the clatter was good
and buxom were the wives and laughing too
what with the love being made. *Could,* and *should*
were yet to be heard, nor *must,* nor *never.*
Then came the maypole, the best thing *ever.*

Stability

We shall stay, just as you say, dear
love, though each of our children
and their children, though our friends
have all gone away. Though Lou
at the liquor store, who delivered,
who cashed our checks for decades
and who cried the day my father died
has himself gone away, and Frank
the mailman and Joe the mailman
have each gone away and Colette
the letter carrier is going away too
who comes through the kitchen door
to hide my presents for you
and listened to my jokes
until the bosses said no more.
Though the fuel guy is going away
to the company of gray Floridians
we will stay here at home, knowing
as we do each creak, rattle and hush.
The rising sun and the setting sun
will be our neighbors. Breezes
when they whistle through our doors
in winter will be welcome till the day
the house falls down, until they blow
the vision from our eyes, our immutable
ties, the powder of our bones away.

Dogwood Blossoms, the Moon, and the Swans

Olsen stays in Florida later each year, deep into spring.
He doesn't see his dogwood blossoming a shock of white,
the leaves on his wine-colored maple bleeding through,
splotches of juniper and lake rippled with sunlight,
any number of mottling things behind the trees in New Jersey.
Even the magnolia flowers and goes without him, the grass
underneath green as the vestments of hope certain Sundays
in a state of grace, when heaven seems close, within reach.

He says there is a moon there too, but does it hang just so,
chalky-white over his condominium in the morning light,
veined and shadowed, flecked with the palest blue,
suggesting the imprint of a person residing within?
Or a hazy mind, not so much like a pearl as is said,
hung by itself in an azure sky fading, valed and pocked.

A fight goes on in Connecticut over the population of swans,
whether there are eight hundred or two thousand, menacing,
and ought to be expelled, or a welcome and beautiful sign.
Whether symbol or thing. Yesterday a pulsing *whirr*
of thirteen swans flew overhead in a muscular determination,
as if oblivious to the content of number, proceeding southwest
at about three hundred feet in an imperfect whiteness, close,
near enough to toast as they flew over my Bordeaux.

A Picture of Trees in Williamstown

And there along the dialectic
where I love you, Pissarro's *Trees*
in Williamstown, a decomposition.

It lasts, this pointillist picture,
fifty-three years now, things as they are,
the way it always is, a vision—

new and of a billion billion parts,
each one lit, or of light. The cars
and the trees, the squirrels

and I among the dissolutions
on Western Avenue in Albany
not two days later, every numinous

flying-by or phenomenal thing
coming apart into color and light.
I stood alone waiting on your porch

in a permanent afternoon—everything
molecular and quick. The staying power
of *to know,* the way the trees, the cars

and streets and animals and I cannot,
alive together in the Great Dissolving
as we are cannot, will never die.

The Picnic in Another Century

—A Critique of Modern Poetry

I
On a blanket from her dormitory,
at Thatcher Park your grandmother and I
with oranges and cigarettes, Chablis
and hearts for a moment under the sky
lay down together once upon a time
in a day of absolute clarity.
Cf. Edouard Manet, *cf.* Seurat—
Omar Khayyam, *cf. The Rubaiyat.*

II
Divigational, he said, *didactic,*
seeming to mean *indirect, preachy.*
Complaining of Donne, *he's an ecstatic—*
excise, cut down, no more commas—trust me,
image, image, imagery, imagiste.
One hundred years of Modern Poetry:
no Horace, or Pope, Dryden or Byron—
no ideas but in things streams on the chyron.

III
Cf. sublime: nothing is higher than—
Herrick and Marvell, *cf.* Catullus.
As twilight hastened and the daylight ran
I read to her from Cavalier poets
while feeding her cherries and marzipan.
With hell below and heaven above us,
she gave me a stocking and I kept it—
for all that semester, I slept with it.

Amateur Nights

We lived the honor of our lives
to hear your bell, awaken and run.
Muscling you in, jostling
your wheelchair. To crash
at the doorjamb bungling it—
honored as we were we failed
or mostly so. We could not do it,
get you down the hall in time
though here in proper measure,
endless love, remembering
your will to certain privacies,
things you would not speak of
even as you died, we leave the rest,
here at the threshold of your pride.

Crossing the Mountain

Time passes swiftly and opportunity is lost.
— Evening Gatha

She posed on the steps of the capitol
in the season of first lovely things, grapes
not yet wine, time yet to be powerful.
A burgeoning love in the cityscapes,
everything new, everything bountiful.
First crab cakes at Keeler's, first flan, first crepes.
State Street and Washington Park, Saratoga,
first of the East, first visions, first yoga.

Of the fruit trees and work, sickness and health,
petals fall first, then leaves—it all flies by.
The River of Time—by guile nor by stealth,
you cannot step into it twice, though you try.
Days of wine and poverty, days of wealth,
having and holding, one of you will die.
You take to your bed, abject, forsaken,
soon you will—*you must strive to awaken.*

Severed from every joy, every splendor,
sometimes there is anger, sometimes regret.
You may speak sometimes, even pray to her.
Crossing the Mountain of Grief, you forget.
Forget again, then again remember,
forever in her thrall, shadow and debt.
First sorrow, first hectoring doom,
even in dreams you cry out to her tomb.

City of Sighs

As between aspiration and perfection.
Common and singular. Inventiveness
and execution. It can hardly be said now:
high and *low. The Stones of Venice*
sits open on the table all winter long
getting dustier. Decorative, meaningful.
As between important and entertaining.
Apt, instructive, nice, necessary, neat.

He has been to Venice twice. At thirty.
At sixty. As between painters and sailors,
and poets: a thousand distinctions of kind
in the light and the sea and the word—
La Serenissima: it is a poem to that effect.
As between youth in a bar near closing,
a sort of Cyrano, poems on the fly, on fire,
ashtrays full of cocktail napkins charred
beyond a use or benefit, and this old age.

He saw, did Ruskin, something to prefer
in the Gothic mind, a rough attainment
to a repetitive refinement. There is a bridge,
palace to prison. This is the Bridge of Sighs.
In *Piazza San Marco* the setting sun,
shades of peach. As between Heaven and soul.
He is glad to have had a little joy, some hope—
after evening *passeggiata,* everyone goes home.

My Proofreader Has Died

My proofer is dead, dear friends. Fifty years,
from *Paralysis in Dubliners* (B+), collegeboy
poetry, *Yeats in the Whirl of History* (B).
The Sixty-Second Tactical Airlift Squadron
Minutes (nineteen seventy-three), polemics
of too many years in politics or business. Now,
as then to my shame, look what I have done—
more about me, less about her as in that selfish
decade upon decade. See it if you can
and understand what will one day be lost to you
one way or the other. Poems, good or bad
for someone to go breathless over or suppose
the next will get you there. In whimsy or in distance,
how she measured out her words, praise or critique
as you might too have done had you only taken
just the minute more, the thirty seconds more
to speak your empty words harmoniously or look
beyond your meaningless accomplishments,
your precious vignettes and monographs
to say goodnight alone in time, to weep or smile
as you are blowing kisses to her photograph.

Forty-seven Years of Sunset

Into the hole the sun sinks in
goes the cove, first losing its glaze,
gone to a cloudy sheen in winter.
Only I remain, officer of lights,
neglectful for a little while.
Lush or barren, trees along the ridge
in a flare-up, pink and gold go in,
blaze and ridge—I have stayed here.
The pines at the end of the street,
street and pines—on a starless night
even the sky falls in, struggle
and merit, failure and accident,
design. Thirteen thousand times, two,
heartbeats and breath and desires.

Still, You Stay

Changing and the same, still
you stay. At twenty, at seventy-three.
Of every age and state
the images remain—the cycles
of our seasons. As if still

we could walk into Knapp's.
Into Knapp's for a ten-cent beer,
every third one free. Typewriter
clacking, your cigarette dangling,
smoke in your eyes, too young

to hope—what could be more than this?
You didn't know, did you?
You smiled on the way
up the stairs, returning
from whatever task or chore,

red-cheeked from winter
or pale with the photos of swans,
the dozens and dozens,
all of the homesick swans
in our springs and our winters of swans.

We Left Our Home of Fifty Years

One way and the other.
I have since spelled backwards *dlrow*
a hundred times for doctors probing
my every incapacity. *Our home is gone,
my refuge.* I have said, half-joking,
après nous le feu, après nous le déluge.
As if it could have been another way, as if
we could have left unscathed but alone.

Tick-infested squirrels command the rafters
now, one may suppose, and chew at the wires.
You hear them after you have gone to bed
as they gnaw their way or scurry
under thunder in the eaves. You fear the fire
as mice eat the cat food or haul it off
to store in the walls, the gray little thieves.

There is the rocking banister, decrepit appliances,
seasonal leaks, galloping finances. Rotting steps
to the deck, the whistling drafts, the switch to gas,
two buried cats. I left deliberately
without a backward look, no stake
in outcomes there or much there to care about—
relieved. The heat here is warm, residents friendly
yet still I awaken fretting, still I awaken grieving.

Oakridge Oregon/Happy Hour

I. Oakridge Oregon
— Found, *The New York Times*, adapted

Above the fog line
and below the snow line
with herds of elk
in the surrounding hills
the town offers a peaceful beauty.
Residents say it is a perfect place
to live, except for the lack of jobs.

II. Happy Hour

Out beyond the empty
lumber yards each morning
elk are snorting
in the standing woods.
When you are gone
for only little bits of time
sunset glows a little
earlier each day.
When you are gone
for far too long
evening is a lurid circus
tent of noise. The clowns
go taunting me in city makeup
deep into the night.

Transcendent at the Arbor Inn Motel

There is to the ice machine latency.
Into the bucket sounds in the hallway,
a muffled shout and *shh* awaken me
not from sleep, but from dreaming.
Where everything is true at once
and I am old and I am young,
at one with revelers. I've had fun:
woke up in Cleveland in 1973
with unfamiliar car keys and whisky,
a little fogged-in. Nothing for me
here in the night-laughs now.
Think of the requisites for wisdom:
a question, a questioner, propinquity.
Disposition, a little remembering.
Restraint. In another room
there is a couple making love.
Not restraint, composure.
That, a little grace, some seasoning—
I am wishing them well, not listening.

Tillman's Ravine

The way you are firm, the way you are yielding,
the give in the floor of the woods is like you.
Loam and rock, accretions of silence, a dignity
burnished here, darkened there. Watching you sleep,
everything seems to persist without measuring,
as if there is nothing to fight, nothing to fear.
Hearing them, murmuring breaths in your dream,
I am going too, riding toward Buttermilk Falls
on your bed with you, under these dapples,
this unlikely, mottled light, gazes at sun, afterlight,
signs. You are clenching your eyes, you start
like a crow in an interval of want or of caution,
perched above an ever deepening, etched trough,
a watercourse, deep, unreachable things.

My Favorite Dream Last Night

That dream again last night.
Flying off a sunny mountaintop
down into clouds as white as Han Shan's beard
but grasping for her in my sleep
jerking awake with a fist full of darkness
no dream.

As we watched the train approach the Salem station
I retreated further back behind the yellow line
you were right about that
I was more afraid of jumping
than of being pushed.

All this introspection
puts me in a confusing metaphorical situation
if I drive your car into the garage
and roll the heavy door down to the floor and lock it
if I get into the trunk with all my sleeping pills
a flashlight and a quart of Jim Beam
if I pull the lid down over me
why would I cry out to her
why would I scream?

And When I Reach for You Again

It is before the rocks have fallen from the hills.
Before the ticks have closed the forests
and the unimagined populace has risen-up
so utterly true—its grainy officialdom
come fallen from the hills in pieces of men,
closing our acropolis and pantheon.

And when I reach for you again
beyond that bare declivity
the drug of my sleep will stultify my limbs
and in each murmur a throttled scream
for it is in my dream I reach
as if to cross these rocks without limbs,
voice, certitude or even mind
in this numbed predicament.

It is before the breach of promises and hope,
before we can no longer tease our progeny
with pretty words into an endless spring—
before we bring them out from under desks
in lurid classrooms, let them know the reason
for this ache and anguish, this withering blight,
that all the rocks are fallen from the hills
and there is nothing left to fear, nothing left to fight.

Psych Ward

If you admit to certain ideations
they will take your shoes away.
Cut the cords out of your hoodie
and the loud men picking fights
loud women picking fights
the red-faced screaming people
slamming doors, *cris des coeurs*
all through the nights
the heart is sometimes yours.
They may not tell you
when you sign the paper
you are theirs for life
theplasticforkandknifetheblaring
idiotic television common room
and scrunched-up faces maybe
on the bossy matrons as they let you
sign a pencil out remind you—*life*.

Tough Love

Lurking on the tongues of friend or parent
like surrender—last-stand shibboleth,
slant rhyme from the marketing department
dissembling for the last ten thousandth time
to snare you in the devil's argument.
All your water cooler friends will tell you,
every casual acquaintance waiting
for the coffee to brew. Shit-house lawyers,
reed-chewing hillbilly philosophers.
Keepers of the books profane and sacred
say it stone-faced in accommodation,
tired priests, gurus in abdication, swamis,
hotlines, robots—none dare call it hatred.

Agostino's Birthday Party

Cent' anni. Raising up my water glass
to Agostino. *One hundred years,*
amico mio, this will be my wish for you.
And though there are those many centuries
of Stoicism in his blood, he tells me *No.*
Your wish is nothing but a curse—enough.
Agostino does not even know his age,
the eighties bad, the nineties worse.
My wife is dead, my children gone,
my teeth and bones are powder.
All my dreams are for the hearse
and Annabelle walks by, her squeaking
walker. He hears again and sort of bows—
Let me go and get some oil for you,
Miss Anabelle, this is all I have to give.
You make me want to live, dear Agostino,
Agostino says, *Me too.*

In the House of Halfway Home

Forty percent of us died.
The overseers kept it from us
as to why. The overseers lied.
And there in Sussex County
where they stacked them up
like so much firewood—
they would if they could.
Nick fell down
and broke his crown, Elaine
came tumbling after. *Jesus.*
I forget his name, the one
who could not hear or speak
who coughed and wheezed
and crapped all through the night.
I could hear him in the shower
crying for his life and clinging to it
in the bathroom we shared.
They had to leave him on the rug
eleven hours by his bed—
the undertaker said he had no room
for more. By then, God help me
all I thought was no more pissing,
no more urine on the floor.

Immanence

What is the part of a thing that is thing?
What is the part of a thing that is space?
In the solid, worth, in the ethers, grace—
I am a spirit, people say, seeing it.

In air and earth and fire and water
our heavenly bodies abide. In iron
and wood, the breath of a billion years.
In each winged and soaring, swooping thing.

Little more than tides, tugged at by the moon
we arise from long nights. After eons, still
we swell, filling the surround with our solidity,
sometimes iron and wood, fire and air ourselves.

I am a spirit, people say, cursing dawn,
irked at the too-soon birds, a day of work, the trod
and drudge of it, the heave and pull and burn and melt,
air and iron, potency and act—less known, more felt.

The Woman Who Hated Her Name

Annabelle, sit.
Until they tie her to her chair
with a bedsheet—all the overseers
screaming at her, *Annabelle, sit.*
And she is drooling *Pater Noster*
on the floor, and she is drooling
Ave, Ave on her *Pater Nosters,*
hail! Annabelle is drooling
Mary on her *Holy Ghosts*
but Annabelle sits.
She waits for *Jeopardy!* Waits
for *Wheel of Fortune* after that,
this is her favorite game show.
Annabelle has long been waiting
since she came to hate her name so.

Annabelle Gets a New Bed

Look behind, not ahead, Seneca said,
an admonition against jealousy.
In places where the beds are bad,
floors hard—bedsprings sprung
and sleep uneasy,
dreams come to falling
deep into the pit of sharp objects,
the chasm of aching bones.

Poor Annabelle, slumped in her chair.
Over her walker—Annabelle slumps,
head-hung and sleepy, hardly there.
The mattresses slide, is the thing—
out over the edge. You fall out of bed
and the mattress falls too,
all of its flimsy ounces come toppling
down over you.

And the matrons will run
to the rescue, some faster, some slow—
lilt and patois in the middlest of night.
They are rubbing their eyes,
rubbing twelve hours out of their eyes,
husbands and children and home.
Annabelle gets a new bed after this—
it's free, one of the pleasures of hospice.

Agostino Wants for Answers

His chair is foremost of residents.
Agostino has questions. He dozes
through all the guest hosts,
gets stuck even on Trevi Fountain.
Tuscany eludes him, and the Adriatic,
Siena, Firenze, the Dolomite Mountains.
I am chef, says Agostino, remembering that.
Maracaibo, Barbados and *Halifax.*

Make any channel you want
he tells me each night,
Jeopardy! just barely begun.
This is no way to live, my friend.
I do not have a gun. I do not,
he says, not *I don't. Will you get me one?*
I tell him I won't. *I was chef, I was chef*
on big ships. Do not touch the women.

I tell him each night of the host,
he is dead. I like Alex Trebek,
poor Agostino says. *What has happened*
to my check, who is boss here?
Your son stole your check,
I tell Agostino. *Maybe it is lost.*
I tell Agostino. I tell him again,
Miss Hazard is boss.

Reading Cicero on Old Age

It is only loneliness, not malaise
I write you in, after another slog
incredulous and wondering
at the same unlikely claims of freedom.
He is released, he says, from the chains
of his body, from the madness of youth,
perfectly at peace with contemplation
and his scrolls, with things in moderation.

Pleasure seems a momentary thing.
Pain seems a momentary thing too.
Even to endure in a time of crisis seems
fleeting—moments of fear and anxiety,
moments in a state of waiting, a diffused,
forgetting mind, a strange world, certainty
or doubt a brief episode one way or the other.
A near future or a far one, utterly elsewhere.

When there is no crisis but I am lonely
or in malaise, here I am with Cicero, my mind
settling sometimes on a diffused light, passing by,
going away, disappearing. Not in malaise tonight
it is just that I am lonely. I am reading Cicero again
on old age in a strange world. I am writing to you
because there is no one, no one left I wish to speak to.

Under Moonlight, Missing Her

Pins in the drapes, a ballast of shot,
duct tape, silk eyeshades—
you cannot hide the moon you tides,
you thousand-year cycles, you *result*.
Laws made you, ineluctable histories.

You in the presence of force, take heed.
Victory, tragedy—these things pick you.
You sleep and awaken, pacing the floor
under moonlight, *feeling* their will—

it is what you see oh toy, plaything
of inconsiderate beings. This moon,
chemistry, accident, contraries. Tossed
into amusing predicaments, a bug

among children, lost and subsumed,
it is fitting you walk the floor—
lifted from dreams, taken
alive. This is to belong, this is to see

in the nighttime again the unpainted
canvas of days. Into the glare
of tomorrow, the shades of the past.
A picture in moonlight her curious,
her mutable ways.

A Healthcare Naif at the Slot Machines

Loretta don't need no stinking science,
she of the multiple falls on her watch,
of unassailable self-confidence,
who sneaks me some Guinness, a little scotch.
She whose hymns sung over the vacuum
pierce like an icepick my afternoon sleep,
She of the loud TV in the rec room,
of magazines, lewd, sensational, cheap.
She above plague, she of dead relatives,
subtle tattoos, religiosity,
speaking in tongues, only superlatives.
Loretta enjoys immortality—
enjoys Friday nights in the casinos,
maskless and stupid in the Poconos.

In the Garden at Montepulciano

Agostino is dreaming the Duomo
there on the bench of his faltering mind
in the church he has long left behind him,
in the garden at Montepulciano.
Dreaming the night will be endlessly kind,
the campanile bells *pianissimo.* Clear the water,
crusty the bread, soft the *vino nobile rosso.*
Let the trees keep flowering deep into spring,
the Baptist is long beyond wondering.
Down from his triptych, down from his altar,
from all the bell towers of Tuscany.
Palace and pulpit, from flowering trees and bare,
come back from your shameless wandering
oh Baptist, come down. Down on the light
of your medieval years, your heavenly idyll.
To the Garden at Montepulciano, bring bread,
water and wine. Bring time for Agostino.

How Claudia Got a Lifetime Sentence

Johnny Nolan has a patch on his ass
Kids chase him
                    — Lawrence Ferlinghetti

Even Miss Hazard is mean to Claudia,
what with her shouts for more water,
her crying for salt, her hassling pleas.
Crap in her room, her cantaloupe knees
that have to be drained, kinks
in her oxygen hose. How it's hot,
how it's cold, her need for more paper
to clean up her nose. The reddish
or grayish or yellowish ooze,
rivulets, bumps and eruptions.
She called Miss Hazard the b-word last year,
blind with pain, out of her mind
in a frenzy of mental disorder, wet pants,
canker, bleeding bedsores, u.t.i., bad teeth.
The cancer she hadn't been told about yet.
Fate, stench, a bad disposition,
Raynaud's syndrome and heartache,
a moustache, edema, a tic—
Miss Hazard has had enough of it.
Claudia has a patch on her ass.
Kids chase her.

Gleaning

— for my late and former housemates

They come in battalions to clean out the rooms,
empty enough already. Nieces and nephews
and daughters and sons, gathering the shards,
leavings of the reaper. Squadrons and klatches
and coteries, platoons. Pickers and packers,
sweepers and lifters, stalwarts and drones—
beneficiaries all, being alive. The burdened
by death, the relieved, the giddy and new to it—
the inured. Riddled with shame for their luck,
treasures to toss, junk to keep, bounty
and surfeit, shortfall and dearth. Maybe a car,
probably old. What to salvage, what to be sold,
taken or given. Protected, refurbished,
cherished, hidden. Cried over, laughed at,
despised. All of those photographs down
from those walls—icons of war: uniforms,
picture hats, detritus of all of those lives.
Images taken, in days of sickness or health,
children, and their children, theirs, dusty
in gilded frames, will cover the walls, soon
enough, of the heirs to the leavings of Stephen
and Fire Chief Lou and of Nick, and Elaine.

Resilience

This is to pray to a God
when you cannot believe,
to call upon hidden powers.

Ten thousand years the stream,
through the rock of a billion
it flows, carving its name, *Will*—

this is to rest beside it.
Kindred with noumena,
with all of those billion years.

Of each of those inches,
of water and stone,
we are the silt.

We have been
in the presence of saints.
This is to revere.

Same and different,
this is to wonder which,
Archons of darkness or light.

To try, to try, to exult, to suffer—
a thousand times knocked down,
a thousand times get up.

At the Bar

Here is Colonel Soupy, here is Harry
from the Vietnam War. Our dear Annie
who worries constantly about the foam
and fills your glass extra to make it right.
Miriam talks to herself, making rhymes
while golden oldies play in four-four time
and all of us remember. All of us,
done with war, Johnny Mathis
singing still in each of our hearts
even if once broken, or broken still.
We trade stories, war stories, if you will,
Miriam too, leaving the hard parts out.
Most leave by seven, all of us by eight—
at home and alive, savoring our fate.

Opposite Day

> *Where there is a reconciliation*
> *there must first have been a sundering.*
> — James Joyce

Around the table at the Memoir Club
we fall upon solitude. *Man's best friend*
says the fisherman, his memories
a little pouch of fishing flies he brings,
objective correlatives—*To be alone*
is not to be lonely. Sometimes,
I am thinking, *sometimes*.
I am thinking of Boethius in prison,
of his wet, his stinking straw, his fall—
his *Consolation of Philosophy,*
second order topics in a runaway of mind
at a meeting, looking for society.
Thinking of outrageous fate, a subject,
really, for the *Socrates Café,* our club
for philosophy. Of a woman there,
she of a certain age as are all of us here,
women and men, fishers and philosophers.
And of the Fire Captain too, dead from the YMCA
in an explicit harmony of bodywork and plague,
of breakfast each day with his fellows—
the *Y* for God's sake, where you go to stay alive.
I am thinking of this catalogue of ache.
There is the Bocce Club. Maybe I will go tomorrow.
I am thinking—where there is a consolation
there must first have been a sorrow.

Prayers into Darkness

Each night I pray in disbelief, a child
at bedtime, begging for a preference.
Fear has gotten hold of me
and superstition, the old arguments
all undone, and I am pleading for an edge
for me and for my people, our little tribe,

my wife of five decades, upon whose death
I went to bed for a year and a half, to find
there is no cure, nor pills enough for grief,
for all the twisted ways we come to see
upon a rupture of a certain kind, no church,
no psych ward, not the tincture of time.

There is a woman at our book club, crazy
as she is from loss and hurt—who cannot cease
her speaking out of turn or keep in mind
whatever silly book we've come to fuss about
and still I have not prayed for her nor she for me—
what can it mean, this thing from which I am not free?

Homecoming

In the dream I dreamed of you,
you came home. Japanese snowbells.
Cornus mas (drupes). Doves,
a cardinal. Doves, doves.
Nova zembla. White azaleas,
blossoming, shined upon mightily.
Everything red, everything white
like the roses, nine and nine.
The little Petrarchan boat
I made for you, in my binge
of Pombal and Segovia—the red
and the white. The coffee-stirrer
strakes, toothpick mast,
button helm (my only
white shirt). The cherry-pink of it,
all of the red and the white.
Silent were Olsen's crows
in Olsen's pines. Stopped
dead for a moment
the traffic on West Shore
as into the sea foam
and currents we launched
above dumbstruck fish.

Letters from Carlo

I

Ah, Sophia, evening can be so beautiful here.
Solitude becomes my friend, a respite and sanctuary.
The colors are very rich, the requirements easily met—
no one here to please or to make nervous or tired.
No use in staying calm or being funny or inventive.
Of course, sometimes I forget you are gone.
It is as if you walk my circles with me.

Always,

Your Carlo

The sky a cup of light between the pines
dark with crows, filling with a sunset glow
of rose and violet—there is time,
as night draws near, to make the best of time.
Heaven cannot know the shades of this peace,
the lavender, the summersweet alive
in pinks and white, butterflies in frolic
as I rest the afternoon away,
a witness as the lily blossoms fade,
the lamia disappears with the sun.
The ease of emptiness confuses me.
I do not imagine happier days
nor bring you back to be with me again
by a wonderful trick of conjuring—
I have no desire; night does not haunt me.
I imagine my flesh rotting away . . .

I imagine my bones powder at last,
riding on the simple breezes
scented with a summer of mimosa—
I imagine us, clouds among the pines.

II

It is as if you never left us, dear Sophia,
as if I never got old. I have been finding things I had forgotten,
remembering things, even what few complicated days we had.
I have been listening to our music, Beethoven and Bach,
all of the string quartets, Puccini arias and duets. Brubeck.
Blue Rondo à la Turk still sends me. You still send me.

Embrace,

Your Carlo

Lusciousheart. Dollface.
Wonderer for real, quick.
Walker in actualness, looker
in the two meanings—
seer in the all conditions
nothingness dark, every hue lit
in the billion bright streams.
Reflection, thing shined upon,
Taken away, staying.
Veiled to the impoverished
even to the point of invisibility,
of all existing mysteries one
shape—sign—substance—soul
in her season flowering.

III

Oh, Glamorpuss, the things married people do.
Watching you dress, watching you put on your makeup . . .
all those years you had me believing you wore almost none.
I wonder what led you to drop that charming pretense.
Did you know you became more beautiful year after year?
The girls are hoping they will have such luck over time,
oblivious to the irony. You were, our dear Sophia, so fine.

À tout à l'heure,

CKT

You ride above the earth as if
the leaves won't freeze, as if the purple
dust of lavender will carry on air
with these gone spirits, gone and here.
Without me like the leaves in fall
before they fall unmindful of the coming
gravity. How many more?
You ride as if calamity will wait,
as if the stars will carry on without us.
You do not return to earth like water,
you just ride it like the air on air
without a shadow, periwinkle dust
behind you, trailing dusts, lavender
and soul and shades, hues and auras
glistening in the night, sailing
by my window brilliant in moonlight.

Elegy Song

— for Barbara

Her skin translucent and girlish her breasts—
when she was twenty, her body thrilled me.
And all was so new when first we undressed
in that faltering world. She was so free—
pondering everything new and ancient,
wondering endlessly. Still, she would play:
Descartes she found silly, Ovid prescient,
scaring all of the sophomore boys away.
Her *womanly* form, though, her queenly smile,
things such as these cannot be predicted—
the arch of her brow, the light of her guile
cannot from the young be elicited
nor, catching me staring, her mockery—
at seventy-three, still thrilling, still free.

Tell Me of Your Days

You said a man is what he sees,
a woman what she hears
in an era of etched boundaries,

your slip falling to the floor.
The coo of pigeons,
the infinite, tiny room.

Tell the years to me my absent one,
deep into the witness of your days.
How they are the same, how they differ.

If they are turning, one into the other
like music from the street will turn,
to a noise of exile, an arid, isolate want

and you appear and disappear, sound
and sense until you cannot hear it there
in your attenuated selves, ears, eyes,

mind after matter, matter after mind.
The seasons are time, and time is empty.
As empty as time there is nothing.

When the seasons turn, we are turning too
and they were always turning. With you
into sense, to a deep, kept wisdom,

common laws of everything true,
to a stone of quiet. Without you
into a street of many darknesses.

Drinks with Doctor Gently

> — He says my poems are all sentiment,
> *not believable, fey, over the top.*

I do not like his whisky, single-malt stuff.
He drinks it with soda, for crying out loud.
What next, The Kingston Trio, battery acid
and cheese, *Begin the Beguine, Moonglow?*
Doctor Gently knows but little as to poems,
less as to theory—*savoir faire* is his passion
even as he renders his bloodless lines,
wherein there is no melancholy, no vastation.

In a surround of lovely things go his days,
two Felix Shermans in a prominent place—
creatures of fable on a background of blue
of which he is fond in their golden frames,
blue and blond, they match the table
on which there sit two Joyces and a Pound,
An Eliot, a Proust, each bound in red leather.
Smart-asses all, Doctor Gently says.

And the snow-covered mountain
comes into the room, brightening,
revealing its manly utility, a sign—
solo at evening by the alabaster lamp's light
draped in his sheepskin from New Mexico.
His red leather chair with his Hemingway,
a man's home, and I say so. *My wife is dead
you stupid schmuck.* He raises up his highball,
he wishes me *good luck.*

Cakes and Tea

Painted cakes do not satisfy hunger.
— Zen Master Dogen

Suns will sink down into their own darkness.
Winds rolling down over the mountain snow—
each of us in the end is alone, you know.
In the light of our own lamp, the heat
of our memories, or the cold—test,
plague or delight—make them well.
Leave no heartache. It carries over,

a wound in solitude—reflect:
        Nothing is fleeting.
Failure and triumph return to you.
Do not squander a propitious moment—
        everything is permanent.

To ravage the cakes, to savor the tea,
this is the reason for the ceremony.
Sorrow and joy, suffered or given,
denied or embraced, arise in the chill-dark
of nighttime, again and again. Listen:
We only get older, no one gets younger—
    and pictures of cake do satisfy hunger.

An Essay on Wonder

You will pray sometimes in desperation,
sometimes in hope across the old chasm.
An ancient bet, there is no hedging it—
in every affirmation, its opposite.

Thus the question is it I, or is it other?
It goes to a state—*to behold in awe*
neither knowing it nor not knowing it.
On the Great Matter first humility

then doubt is borne, the recanting
of the visions, an everlasting *No*
as if the strongest, weakest thing
were not desire and desire at war,

fire, fighting fire—a brightening.
Agency and animation—to see,
to aspire and to make, to adhere
and to fall away. But once

beside a lake or stream in sultry air
you saw, or someone saw, a thing divine
glistening on the waters in moonlight
and found it good, and rested there.

The Butterfly Effect

I was borne on wings of not quite yet
above the density of stubborn rock
while ignorant below there passed
my very own winners in a lottery.

So on the day that almost was, the rock
there teetering below the butterfly,
the rock that could not fall. It was not time
despite those mighty, fluttering wings.

And then below the cliff, naked and good
there came two more in love, unluckily
as on that path together they would die
of butterfly and rock and gravity.

To the seventh generation love and luck
between to be and not to be—no one
under soon to topple stones to tell you
in these eons who and when the rock,

who not. If plenty, want, felicity.
Luck, a monarch on wings, if synchronicity.
Near ones to cherish, enemies to curse—
thank you dear time, dear universe.

A History of Faith

All of this darkness. All of this light.
I live alone now, night brings both to me.
Morning does not call my name or symbolize,
I stumble through the aches and creaks
as if the sun were not shining
on my bronze eagle from the old company.
Leaving it was not so hard after a time.
It seemed a pretty pretense I might so arise
as if to be old were just a temporary thing.
It is exactly thus, dear haunted ones,
tremulous and hidden, useless and afraid
but it is nighttime. Have I taken my pills?
Yes, I think so, yes, I believe I have.
Oh, faith: in the remnants of mind
or caverns of a time alone
you see, you hear embodied voices,
fond and knowing after living-out the years
and time seems lucid, and true, and enough.

I Think I Know

— An Essay on Epistemology

Whose words are these—the lovely woods
the snow and horse all come to metaphor?
Of noumenon and gnosis, pilgrim, faith,
of solipsism, comfort to be found,
shared ground on which the citizenry stood
in shared intent and mutual consent
beneath fixed stars. On the declivity
of your truth and mine oppressed, tyranny
of subjectivity and falsity
delicious, buxom siren sucked-on now
in this the mosh pit of our ignorance
and superstition, our sightless, plucked eyes,
seeded intuitions and suspicions
as, blind, our televisions clash by night.

Like a Head Lopped Off

Like a head lopped off. A severing blow.
So usual to lose a mind in the interstices.
Of one become two, comfort, whimsy, grace
all ripped away. Just like that. No ministries
or ministrations, tendings-to nor love enough . . .
religions, fire, spirit, soul, *urstuff*,
psychiatric wards, indomitable will.
Community nor isolation. Just merciful time . . .
time's tincture finds you breathing deeply
silent, grateful and still, hovering
on sleep. Forgetting to pray, forgetting
one unlikely night to remember her.
Death's work is an endless day ending—
all the threads that bind us are of gossamer.

On the Asymmetry of Light

When I was young and staring into space
from a landscape of American dreams
the stars seemed close and I seemed far away,
misaligned under shimmer and moonbeams.
As if the darker parts were permanent,
the stars were close and I was far away.

I met a girl and she met me
and there were fifty years
unwearied and still, or years that seemed so
as I reached into her coma with "The Wild Swans
at Coole" and she reached back to me from light,
from starlight and darkness, said to me *I wuh woo*

and all the stars were close and I was far away
and kissing the bitter salt of her skin.
Staring into space as if there were no years
nor, wander where they will, progeny
and progeny of progeny, three little boys
to turn to in the light of day, to attend upon still.

At the Locus of Old Men

The other Harry at the bar and I
the other face of Nick at the gym
the other Tom and Dick, another
Harry, from the Korean War
Ed the sales guy from Long Island
the other poor Jim, rich William
in their cups or after a few sit-ups
calling it a day admit to it,
it never goes away. None want it gone
the photographs remain above the bed.
Evidence to the contrary
notwithstanding as it might be said
by counsel or the other counsel Steve
who crazed by desire cannot believe
will not believe that she is really dead.

In the Nature of Again

When the beast gnaws
at your viscera again
it is in the nature of *again* to bet
against the beast. In the nature of *again*
to bet against the beast again.
Sure, it will be one day
a bum calculation—but why dwell
on certainties? It is in the *when* more
than the *again* of things, no?

Do not kid yourself—
it is a thing to be afraid of.
Maybe you should dream it worse—
your flesh rotting away, picked dry,
your bones blanched, turning
to powder in the sun, blowing away.
Grain by grain the dust of you on subtlest
of breezes to distances just and unjust
and settling back, you again.

The Water-Walker

What are you thinking, old skinbag—
old moss-antlered man—old sillyboy
not three years since . . .
old voluptuary, faker, old flirt.

Au courant, she does not swim, but walks.
In water just up to her décolletage,
backing and forthing these minutes a day,
proof in its way of a lust for things mortal.
An appetite for life. Hope, diligence, *courage,*
a conquering spirit, alone as she is and wise—
(To live is to hold on. To be and become. To *try*).

Perhaps I'll enchant her one evening.
I shall not make the drinks too strong, a testament
to my trustworthiness. Nor too weak—a sign
of my vigor. Urbanity, suavity, grace.

Reading to her, I'll stay clear of the Cavaliers,
of all Seventeenth Century poems. This lest the tears
reveal me. Fifty years . . . what are you thinking
old skinbag? There is little to say . . . keep your wits,
do not caterwaul so, nor cry, nor stare at le décolleté.

Regarding Spring

Let there be song and dance,
joy among singers and dancers.
A woman has taken a fancy.
Coquette she may be,
giddy with spring,
with spring pulsing so—
spring on the very air.
One mind of it, though,
her mind, and mine
and the season's.

Love Among the Elderly

It is hard to understand the sorrows
when they reappear—
lethargy after splendor, the embrace,
the going away
of ease again as I make my way home
to hover blankly
at a blank computer screen for hours
waiting on daylight.
As if to stare will make for clarity,
aggregate right words
to stanzas worthy of a Cavalier
as pretty phrases fall
blank and obscure. In a time that cannot know
we reach for one another and our name is Hope.

Of Death and Desire

The will to believe. Beach Boys and psychiatrists.
A crucible of fire and ice. Of death and desire,
Wouldn't it Be Nice? And necessary
there in your dark of nights alone
assured by centuries. Of implausible ideas
among photographs and fading memories,
of amorous dreams forgotten too soon—
wouldn't it be nice? Of faith in continuity.
Of beginnings and of goings on, getting up
and getting up again, over and over and of how
you carry her, you carry her wherever you go.
Of hope and desperation, *wanting* is believing it
throughout the turning seasons, knowing it would be
so nice and therefore how it must be so.

The Fountain

There is a fountain on Fifty-first,
near Second. Man-made though it is,
I think my grandson had *satori* there.

Look, I know fountains,
but this boy swooned. As if
seeing it all, finding it good,
and resting. Another being
entirely, asleep in my lap,
deep sighs—a fountain-full.

Of course, it's been dark—
all of the death and separation,
all of the being wrong
in the loudest voice—Saint Paul
on a horse couldn't fix that.

But there is fire at the center of us,
at the center of us, *qi*. You can feel
the heat of it, the way it will flow,
right out of your tingling hands—

splendor and power. Clairvoyant,
you can see tomorrow now: eating
your Cheerios, drinking your juice,
cleaning your bowl
and your glass and your spoon.

That Second of Seeing Just Before Sleep

Nodding off, too soon, another night aspiring
after loveliness or worthiness or animating facts
derived from a compendium of another's dreams,
a perfect knowing just escapes me on the verge
of sleep, falling down a well of light sublime
enough to chase in the singular sanity of abandon.
Every heart of mine evolves into an endless trust
and I begin to tumble after it, everything resolved,
gone before me in its own generous time and seen
as if in reach within these meager lifetimes, real.
Beyond the offerings of all these pages, peace,
and I have lost my place. We shall begin again
tomorrow, where the bookmark has been stuck
in an uncertain way, we start again, another day.

December

The cove will be going to ice, a mirror
in which there is no face, no quickening,
no gleam. The moon will withhold
from its glistening, until there is snow,
enough to make brightness, a glowing
all through the night, a surround,
a kind of softness. One doesn't wonder

just yet, of Buttermilk Falls,
if it has begun its thickening,
become slow, a slurry, seizing up.
I remember my spouse, gone now
these one thousand days.
One does not know, and the roads
will be closed the fifteenth.

One cannot go in this cold.
Until spring supersedes,
everything stays in abeyance.
Buttermilk Falls will fall
unattended, a silvery string
from Tillman's Ravine
to the Flatbrook, remember or no.

Acknowledgments

Journal of New Jersey Poets, "A Picture of Trees in Williamstown," "Tillman's Ravine"

This Broken Shore, "Under Moonlight, Missing Her"

The Stillwater Review, "Opposite Day," "Homecoming," "December" (in another version)

The C C Villager, "Stability," "Still, You Stay," "Crossing the Mountain," "Elegy Song"

Sincerest thanks to my beloved daughters Elizabeth Day Tripi and Susannah Providence Torpey, who got me through the transition; to my dear companion-aide Terry Futcher, who created and sustains for me an atmosphere in which poetry can take place. To Judith Ann Christian, to Jean LeBlanc and all of my friends at The Sussex County New Jersey Writers' Roundtable, my poetry home of twenty years; to its Director Elaine Koplow; to the Betty June Silconas Poetry Center at Sussex County Community College and its Director Scott Humphries for fourteen years of kindness to my poetry.

Back cover photo, Barbara and Chuck Tripi,
Lake George, New York, 2010

Master Ni Does a Peculiar Thing

The water is always refreshed.
The stone in the bowl on the table
has never been dry.
A treatise on practice, a treatise
on growing the stone.
Do not listen to the words
says Master Ni—*watch the feet.*

It was all just a dream.
A walk in the garden tomorrow,
a walk in the garden
the day after that,
in the garden the day after that.
Dans le jardin elle est là.
In the garden she is there.